CHARLIE BROWN'S CYCLOPEDIA

SCIENCE CAN BE SUPER
Sound, Light, and Air

VOLUME · 8 ·

Based on the Charles M. Schulz Characters
Funk & Wagnalls

Photo and Illustration Credits:
AP/Wide World Photo, 53; The Bettmann Archive, 27, 32; Anthony A. Boccaccio/Image Bank, 55; Courtesy Cycle Products Company, Commack, N.Y.; E.R. Degginger/Earth Scenes, 13, 35, 37; Bryce Lee, 14, 20, 22, 24; Lawrence Manning/West Light, 15; Chuck O'Rear/West Light, 39, 40; Margaret W. Peterson/Image Bank, 21; Richard Price/West Light, 17; Diana O. Rasche/West Light, 31; Mary Ellen Senor, 26, 28, 36, 39, 40, 43, 44, 47, 50.

ISBN: 0-8374-0053-8

Part of the material in this volume was previously published in *Charlie Brown's Second Super Book of Questions and Answers*.

Funk & Wagnalls, founded in 1876, is the publisher of *Funk & Wagnalls New Encyclopedia*, one of the most widely owned home and school reference sets, and many other adult and juvenile educational publications.

INTRODUCTION

Welcome to volume 8 of *Charlie Brown's 'Cyclopedia!* Have you ever wondered where echoes come from, or what makes cartoon characters move, or how scuba divers breathe underwater? Charlie Brown and the rest of the *Peanuts* gang are here to help you find the answers to these questions and many more about sound, light, and air. Have fun!

Charlie Brown's 'Cyclopedia
has been produced
by Mega-Books of New York,
Inc. in conjunction
with the editorial, design,
and marketing staff of
Field Publications.

**STAFF FOR
MEGA-BOOKS**

Pat Fortunato
Editorial Director

Diana Papasergiou
Production Director

Susan Lurie
Executive Editor

Rosalind Noonan
Senior Editor

Adam Schmetterer
Research Director

**Michaelis/Carpelis
Design Assoc., Inc.**
Art Direction and Design

**STAFF FOR
FIELD PUBLICATIONS**

Cathryn Clark Girard
Assistant Vice President,
Juvenile Publishing

Elizabeth Isele
Executive Editor

Kristina Jorgensen
Executive Art Director

Leslie Erskine
Marketing Manager

Elizabeth Zuraw
Senior Editor

Michele Italiano-Perla
Group Art Director

Kathleen Hughes
Senior Art Director

CONTENTS

Can you hear the sound of a pin dropping? Probably not. There are all sorts of sounds you *can* hear, though, from the sweet, chirping sound of a tiny bird's song to the big, crashing sound of a brass marching band. How are sounds made, and how do we hear them? Let's find out.

LISTEN TO THE SOUNDS

CHAPTER 1

SOUND AND HOW WE HEAR

What is sound?

Sound is what you hear when something vibrates—moves back and forth quickly. If you stretch a rubber band and twang it, you can see the vibrations that cause the sound. Or try it with a guitar. You can see the vibrations when you pluck a guitar string.

Anything that vibrates makes the air around it vibrate. When the air vibrates, it creates sound waves in the air. Usually you can't see any vibrations when you hear a sound, but the vibrations are still there. Sound vibrations travel through most other materials, as well as through air.

How do we hear sound?

When sound waves enter your ears, they make the insides of your ears vibrate. Inside each ear is a sheet of cells called the eardrum. The sheet is stretched tight, like the skin across the top of a drum. When the sound waves hit the ear-

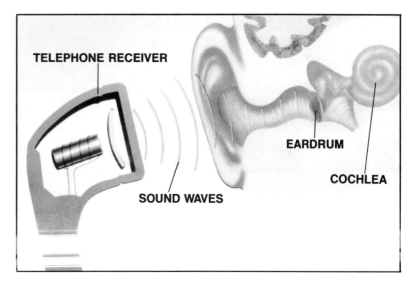

drum, the eardrum begins to move quickly, or vibrate, the way a drum does when it is hit. These vibrations cause three tiny bones in the ear to vibrate, too. The bones' vibrations, in turn, cause vibrations in a liquid that fills the deepest part of the ear. The moving liquid presses on your hearing nerve cells, which pass the message on to your brain, and the sound is heard!

Why are some sounds low and others high?

The sound coming from a vibrating object will be high or low depending on how many sound waves it makes each second. The highness or lowness of sound is called pitch. A low sound, like that made by a foghorn, has slow-moving waves. A high sound, like that made by a whistle, has fast-moving waves. The lowest sounds that most people can hear have about 20 vibrations each second. The highest sounds people can hear have about 20,000 vibrations per second. Some animals, such as bats and dolphins, can hear very high sounds—those with more than 100,000 vibrations per second. The scientific word for the number of vibrations per second is *hertz*. It is abbreviated hz. People can hear sounds between 20 and 20,000 hertz.

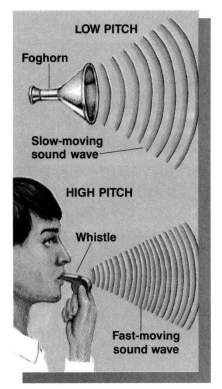

Do sound waves behave differently if it is cold or wet outside?

Yes. Temperature and water affect how fast sound waves can travel. The speed of sound is slower in cold air and faster in warm air. Sound waves that travel in water may move four times faster than they would in air. Think of that! Although water would slow you down if you were trying to run in a pool, sound waves move faster in a pool. Sound waves that travel through solids move about 15 times faster than they would through air!

What are echoes?

Echoes are sounds made by reflected sound waves. If you stand near the wall of your school gym and clap your hands, you hear the sound of the clap. In a moment, you may hear the sound again. That's the echo.

You hear the first sound instantly, as sound waves travel from your hands to your ears, but sound waves travel in many directions at the same time. Some reach the gym wall, bounce off it, and return to your ear as reflected sound—the echo.

Can echoes be bad?

Echoes can be annoying in auditoriums or concert halls. Sometimes when an orchestra or band is playing, many echoes travel in all directions. The reflected sound that mixes with the original sound can form one continuous sound. If this happens, the music will sound muffled or unclear, as if you were wearing a hat pulled over your ears. Some concert halls pad the seats, walls, and floors to absorb, or take in, some of this reflected sound. Then, the audience hears only the original sound made by the orchestra.

How does a band shell use reflected sound?

Some outdoor theaters have been built so that they make use of reflected sound with band shells. They are designed in such a way that the reflected sound is sent directly back to the audience. This way the sound is not lost. Instead, the sound is amplified (AM-pluh-fied), or made louder.

A symphony orchestra performs in the band shell at the Hollywood Bowl in California.

Sound Waves at Work

How does a stethoscope help a doctor listen to your heart?

A stethoscope lets the doctor listen with both ears. Before stethoscopes were invented, a doctor had to listen to a heart by pressing one ear against the patient's chest. Now doctors hear heartbeats better by using both ears.

A stethoscope has two listening pieces to help the doctor hear different kinds of sounds. The small disk piece is good for listening to very low-pitched sounds. The large disk piece is good for listening to higher sounds. The sounds travel from the listening pieces through rubber tubes to the doctor's ears. The next time you go for a checkup, ask the doctor to let you listen to your heart with the stethoscope.

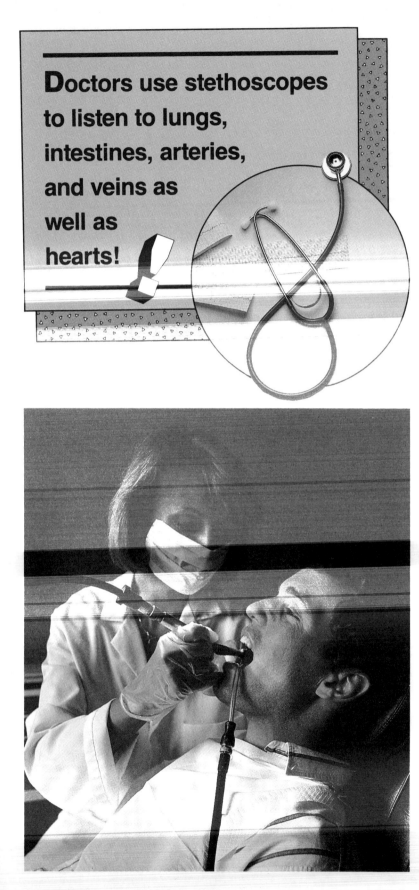

Doctors use stethoscopes to listen to lungs, intestines, arteries, and veins as well as hearts!

Can doctors use sound to see inside your body?

Yes. Doctors use sound called ultrasound. Ultrasound vibrates above the 20,000 hertz region, where we can't hear. These sound waves can be sent into the human body. The sound waves travel through liquids such as blood and water differently than through solids such as bone and muscle. Doctors can look at the different organs inside the body when the waves form an image, or picture, on a special screen. Doctors use ultrasound to make sure an unborn baby is growing in a healthy way inside its mother.

How do dentists use ultrasound?

Dentists can use ultrasound to clean teeth. An ultrasonic scaler vibrates to remove hard deposits, called tartar, on the teeth. Who ever thought that teeth could be cleaned using sound?

CHAPTER 2

Strike up the band. We're ready to hear the blare of the trumpets, the call of the bugle, and the rat-tat-tat of the drum! Join the *Peanuts* marching band and orchestra for a music lesson that can't be beat! There will be lots of instruments to read about along the way.

MUSIC TO YOUR EARS

THE SOUND OF MUSIC

How do musical instruments make sounds?

All musical instruments make air vibrate, but they don't all do it in the same way. Some have strings that vibrate. Others have small pieces of wood, called reeds, that vibrate. With some instruments, the vibrations come from the player's lips. Drums, cymbals, and xylophones (ZIGH-luh-fones) vibrate when somebody strikes them.

Most musical instruments are made so that the player can control how high or low the sound will be.

PIANO

How does a piano make sounds?

Most pianos have 88 keys. There are 52 white keys and 36 black keys. Attached to every piano key is a hammer. This is a piece of wood covered with a felt pad. When you press a key, the hammer hits a small group of metal strings. Most pianos have 230 strings.

The pitch of each string depends on how long and thick the string is and how tightly it is stretched. Short, thin strings have a higher pitch than long, thick strings. The tighter you stretch a string, the higher its pitch will be. Some of the strings are wrapped with wire to make them vibrate more slowly, which creates lower sounds.

PLAY IT AGAIN, SCHROEDER.

In 1935, a giant-sized piano was built in London. Its longest string was 9 feet long. That's probably more than twice your height!

GUITAR

How does a guitar make music?

A guitar has strings that make sounds when you pluck the strings with your fingers or strum them with a pick. The strings are stretched across a pear-shaped box. Without this box, the strings would make a very faint sound. The box amplifies the sound, makes it louder.

The pitch of a guitar note depends on two things: the thickness and the tightness of the strings. In that way, a guitar is like a piano. On a guitar, however, you can change the pitch by pressing a string with your finger. When you do this, you are cutting short the part of the string that vibrates. In a way, you are making the string shorter. Banjoes and ukuleles (you-kuh-LAY-leez) work in much the same way.

TUNING SCREWS

STRINGS

SOUND HOLE

BRIDGE

SOUND BOARD

VIOLIN

Does a violin work the same way as a guitar?

Not quite. A violin has strings like a guitar. When you play a violin, you control the pitch by pressing on the strings—as you do with a guitar. Instead of plucking the strings to make them vibrate, however, you rub a bow across the strings. The bow is a wooden stick with horse-hairs stretched between the ends. Sound vibrations are made when the hairs rub on the violin strings. Some violinists may occasionally pluck the violin strings like those of a guitar to get interesting sounds.

Imagine playing a violin under water! Mark Gottlieb did it as a stunt in 1975 in Olympia, Washington. He played Handel's *Water Music!*

WIND INSTRUMENTS

What is a wind instrument?

A wind instrument is any instrument that makes a sound when someone blows into it. A horn, a kazoo, and a saxophone are all wind instruments.

A wind instrument has a body made of a long or short tube. When you blow into the instrument, air vibrates inside the tube. The longer the tube, the lower the pitch. Most wind instruments have push buttons on, or holes in, the tube. That's where you put your fingers when you play the instrument. When you press a button or uncover a hole, the pitch changes because the space left for the air to vibrate in changes.

There are two main kinds of wind instruments. They are called brass and woodwind.

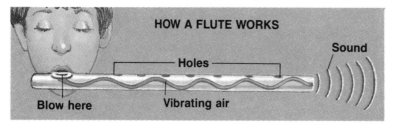

HOW A FLUTE WORKS

Holes

Sound

Blow here

Vibrating air

PEANUTS MARCHING BAND

What are brass instruments like?

Bugles, trumpets, cornets, trombones, tubas, French horns, and sousaphones are brass instruments. They all have long tubes that are folded or curled around to make the instrument easier to carry. Brass instruments are made of brass.

When you play a brass instrument, you press your lips together and make a buzzing sound like "p-f-f-f-t" as you blow into the tube. When you go "p-f-f-f-t," your lips vibrate. This makes the air in the instrument vibrate. The pitch of the sound depends on how quickly or slowly you vibrate your lips.

How are woodwind instruments played?

Woodwind players blow air across one or two thin pieces of wood called reeds. Clarinets, oboes, bassoons, and saxophones are played this way. Blowing makes the reeds, and then the air, vibrate. Woodwind instruments without reeds—flutes and piccolos—have a hole in the mouthpiece that the player blows air across. Blowing across the hole makes the air inside the instrument vibrate. Once, all woodwinds were made of wood. Today, some are made of plastic or metal.

PERCUSSION INSTRUMENTS

What is a percussion instrument?

Percussion instruments are usually struck with sticks, the hand, or mallets to make music. The entire instrument may vibrate, as do cymbals, or part of it may vibrate, as does the skin on the top of a drum.

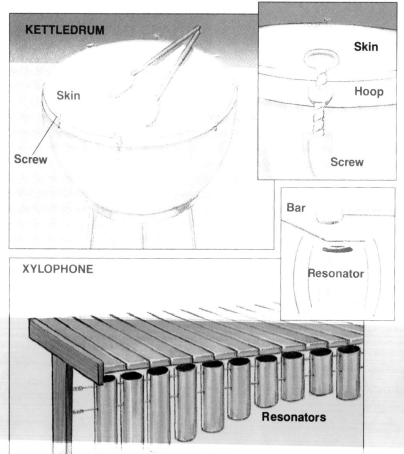

KETTLEDRUM

Skin

Screw

Skin

Hoop

Screw

Bar

Resonator

XYLOPHONE

Resonators

How do they make sound?

When a cymbal is hit, the sound can only be made louder or softer; the pitch cannot be changed. The pitch is changed on a drum by tightening or loosening the skin. Xylophones are instruments with lots of bars. When the bars are struck, a sound is made. The longer the bar, the deeper the sound.

CHAPTER 3

Your eyes need it to see. A camera needs it to take photographs. Movies need it to move. Doctors need it to see inside your body. What is *it*? It's wonderful light!

LIGHTS, CAMERA, ACTION!

LIGHT AND HOW WE SEE IT

What is light?

Light is a form of energy. Like sound, light travels in waves. Light waves vibrate like sound waves, and can have different speeds of vibration. Instead of letting us hear different pitches, however, light waves allow us to see a whole world of different colors.

Each color of light has its own length of wave. Red light waves are long, violet ones are short. The light waves for other colors are in between those two.

Is it true that your eye is like a camera?

Yes, it's true. A camera has a diaphragm (DIE-uh-fram), a ring or plate that gets bigger or smaller to let in the right amount of light. Your eye has an iris that does the same thing. A camera has a lens that focuses the light into a clear picture. Your eye also has a lens to focus the light. In a camera, the light helps to form a picture on film. In your eye, the picture is formed on the retina (RET-ih-nuh), at the back of the eye. The picture is upside down on both the film and on your retina.

How do you see?

You see with your eyes, and also with your brain. First, waves of light pass into your eye and form an upside-down picture on your retina. The retina has special nerve cells on it. When the light hits these cells, they send a "picture message" to your brain. Your brain interprets the message into a right-side-up picture—and you see.

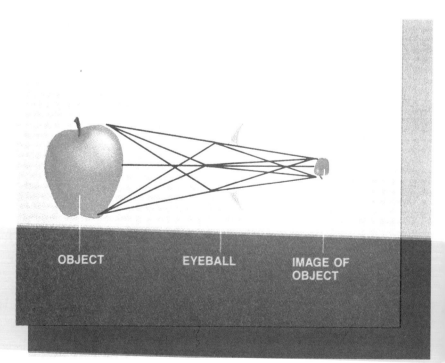

OBJECT   EYEBALL   IMAGE OF
                                 OBJECT

How do eye-glasses and contact lenses help people see better?

When light waves enter the eye, they pass through the curved front end called the cornea. Then they pass through the lens. The cornea and the lens of the eye focus, or aim, the light waves so that **the picture on the retina** will be clear. Some people's eyes cannot do this very well. If an eyeball is too long or too short from front to back, the image will be blurry.

Eyeglasses and contact lenses are extra lenses put in front of the eyes' own lenses. They focus or bend the light waves. Then the waves come together correctly in the eye and form a clear picture.

This painting shows Benjamin Franklin and his invention, bifocals.

How are bifocals different from other eyeglasses?

Regular eyeglasses have one simple lens for each eye. The lens helps a person see either nearby things better or faraway things better. Bifocals have one lens with two parts for each eye. One part helps a person see nearby things better. The other helps a person see faraway things better.

Benjamin Franklin invented bifocals in 1785. Before that time, people who needed glasses to see both faraway and nearby things clearly had to carry around two pairs. With bifocals, however, such people need only one pair of glasses.

LIGHT AT WORK

How does a camera make photographs?

A camera works very much like an eye. Light waves enter the front of a camera through a set of lenses. The lenses focus the light to form a picture on the inside

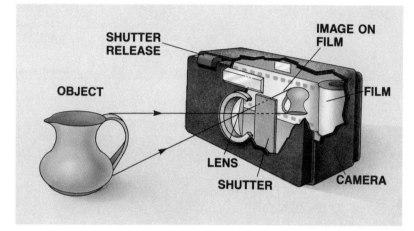

back wall of the camera. To make photographs, you need a roll of film. Photographic film is a strip of plastic coated with special chemicals that change when light hits them. The camera is made to hold part of the roll of film against the back wall of the camera. When you press the shutter release, light comes into the camera. The light waves shine on the film. They change the chemicals so that a picture will appear when the film is developed.

How is film developed?

When you take your film to be developed, the person you give it to sends it to a laboratory. There, the film is taken into a darkroom and unrolled. The developing has to be done in the dark because light would ruin your pictures. The film is dipped into a tank of liquid chemicals. These chemicals change the colors of the chemicals on your film in such a way that pictures are formed. These pictures are called negatives. A negative shows the objects in the picture with the right shapes but the wrong colors. If black-and-white film is used, the blacks will appear white, and the whites will appear black. If color film is

COLOR NEGATIVE

used, the colors will be very different from those in the finished photograph.

Next, each negative is placed in a machine called an enlarger. The enlarger holds the negative and shines light through it for a few seconds, projecting the picture onto a piece of photographic paper. Photographic paper is coated with chemicals on one side. The paper remains blank, but the light causes invisible changes in the chemicals.

Next, the paper is placed in a pan of liquid chemicals. These liquids change the chemicals on the paper. Slowly, as the chemicals change, the picture appears, and your photograph is finished.

BLACK AND WHITE NEGATIVE

How can X rays take a picture of a person's insides?

X rays are like light waves, but they are much shorter and have greater energy. Scientists have built machines, called X-ray machines, that shoot beams of X rays, just as flashlights shoot beams of visible light. When light waves hit a person, they bounce off. When X rays hit a person, however, they go right through—just as light goes through a piece of glass. Light waves and X rays behave differently when they hit a person, but when either light waves or X rays hit a piece of photographic film, they behave the same. Both kinds of waves change the chemicals on the film. To make an X-ray picture of a person's insides, an X-ray machine shoots rays through the person onto a piece of photographic film. Like the sound waves used in ultrasound pictures, X rays travel differently through the liquid and solid parts of the body. When the film is developed, it shows a shadowy picture of the bones and other organs inside the body.

SOME PEOPLE ARE BEAUTIFUL INSIDE AND OUT.

The man who discovered X rays, Wilhelm Roentgen (RENT-gun), didn't understand what they were. That's why he called the rays *X!* X is a common mathematical symbol for an unknown!

What is a CAT scanner?

A CAT scanner is a special kind of X-ray machine. CAT is a word made from the initials of the words *computer assisted tomography*. Words made from the initials of other words are called acronyms (ACK-ruh-nimz). Acronyms help people save time in talking, writing, and remembering by changing a group of big words into one little word.

A person who is going to have a CAT scan is placed into the machine, which looks like a giant tube. The X rays from the CAT scan shoot through the person onto a plate, and then the tube is turned a little. More X rays are sent through the body. Then the machine turns again. The machine continues to scan until it finally gets back to its starting place. Regular X rays just shine waves through one side of a person. The CAT scan shines rays through a person in a complete circle. Because so much information is gathered by a CAT scan, a computer must be used to help make sense out of the hundreds of pictures it takes. These CAT scan pictures are much clearer than those produced by regular X-ray machines.

A technician operates a CAT scanner.

MOVIES AND CARTOONS

What makes movies move?

If you look at a piece of movie film, you can see that it is just a long series of photographs on a plastic strip. Each photograph is a tiny bit different from the one just ahead of it and the one behind it. If the film is of someone running, jumping, or diving, you can see that the arms and legs are in different positions in different pictures. When you show the film in a projector, the projector flashes the pictures on a screen one at a time, but they flash on very fast—usually 24 pictures per second. When the pictures flash by that fast, your brain can't tell that your eyes are looking at many separate photos. You think you are looking at only one picture—a picture that moves.

A-choo! Here's a strip of film showing a sneeze.

Who invented movies?

No one knows for sure. In the 1880s and 1890s, many people were working on ways to make moving pictures. In 1891, Thomas Edison, the inventor of the light bulb, built the first kinetoscope (kin-ET-uh-scope). This was a cabinet with a peephole. Inside were reels of film that turned. A person looked into the peephole to see the movie. Some people believe that Edison's helper, Thomas Dickson—not Edison—invented the kinetoscope.

THOMAS EDISON AND HIS KINETOSCOPE

How are cartoon movies made?

Cartoon characters are just drawings, and they can't move. It is possible, however, to play a trick on people's eyes so that it looks as if the characters are moving. This is called cartoon animation. To create animation, artists draw thousands of pictures on separate clear plastic sheets called cels. Each picture shows a character in a slightly different position.

For each scene, the artists paint a background. One or more cels are put on top of the background. The combination is photographed by a special movie camera, which takes only one picture each time a button is pressed. (A regular movie camera keeps taking one picture after another.) Then the cels just photographed are taken off the background. The next picture is placed on the background. It is only slightly different from the first picture. The second picture is then photographed. In fact, one picture is taken for each tiny bit of movement a character makes. When the film is shown through a movie projector, the characters appear to move.

Cartoon movies can also be made with puppets. They can be animated by moving their bodies in a slightly different position for each picture.

CHAPTER 4

What travels faster than sound and comes in all the colors of the rainbow? The answer is right before your eyes—light! With the help of prisms, mirrors, and magnifying glasses, light can do some incredible things. Just watch!

A CHANGE OF DIRECTION

PRISMS

What is a prism?

A prism is a bar of glass with flat sides. A good prism has no bubbles or ripples in it. When a beam of sunlight passes through a prism, the light spreads out into separate beams of color. The colors are the same as those you would see in a rainbow—red, orange, yellow, green, blue, indigo, and violet. A rainbow in the sky is created when light passes through drops of water in the air that act as prisms. Like a prism, a drop of water can change sunlight into separate colored beams of light.

Sunlight creates a wide range of colors when it passes through a prism.

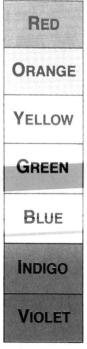

RED

ORANGE

YELLOW

GREEN

BLUE

INDIGO

VIOLET

How does a prism cause a rainbow?

A beam of sunlight is really a mixture of light waves of many colors. As we've already learned, each color of light has its own kind of wave. Red light waves are long, violet light waves are short, and the other colors are in between.

When light waves enter a prism, they bend, and they bend again when they come out of the other side of the prism. The various colors bend by different amounts. Because of this, the colors spread out as they pass through the prism. The colors line up side by side in the order shown here.

THIS IS A REPORT ABOUT A BUNCH OF BAD LIGHT WAVES WHO WERE SENT TO PRISM...

Mirrors and Magnifying Glasses

Why does a mirror show a picture of what's in front of it?

A mirror shows a picture, called a reflected image, because the mirror has a shiny, silver-colored coating behind the glass. The coating does two things:

1. It keeps the light waves from passing through the mirror. Since they can't go through, they bounce back toward your eyes.

2. It makes the mirror *very* shiny. When light waves bounce off a dull surface, they scatter. When the light waves bounce off something shiny, however, they don't scatter at all.

When you stand in front of a mirror, light waves move from you to the shiny mirror. The light waves then bounce right back off the mirror in exactly the same way they hit the mirror. And you see yourself!

How does a magnifying glass make things look big?

A magnifying glass plays a trick on your eyes. It does this by changing the direction of light waves coming from the object you are looking at. The curved surfaces of the magnifying glass bend the waves, and it appears to your eyes that the waves are coming from a big object.

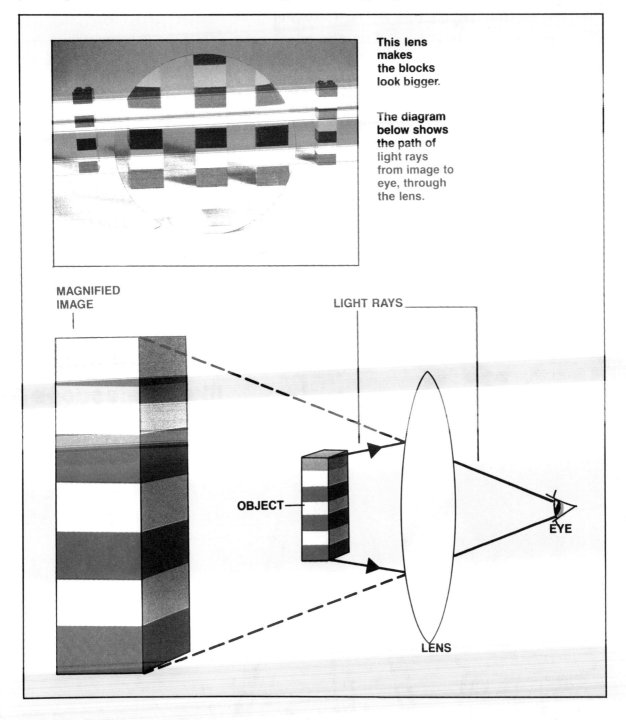

This lens makes the blocks look bigger.

The diagram below shows the path of light rays from image to eye, through the lens.

MAGNIFIED IMAGE

LIGHT RAYS

OBJECT

EYE

LENS

TELESCOPES AND MICROSCOPES

How does a telescope work?

By using a series of lenses, the eyepiece of the telescope makes distant objects look closer. The lenses in the telescope let us see faraway objects that are normally invisible. In fact, the telescope can make these objects appear as if they were right next to us. We can even see planets that are two billion miles away!

GEE, I THOUGHT THE BIG DIPPER WAS A LARGE ICE CREAM SCOOP.

Is a microscope like a telescope?

Yes. It lets us see very small objects that would otherwise be invisible to us. Unlike the telescope, the microscope focuses on objects that are very close to us. One set of lenses makes an enlarged image of the object. Then the eyepiece lenses enlarge the image further.

LASERS AND HOLOGRAMS

What is a laser?

A laser is a machine that shoots a thin, very high-powered beam of light. This beam is called a laser beam. Some laser beams are so powerful that they can burn holes in metal.

Here's a colorful laser light show.

How does a laser work?

A laser beam comes from a laser tube. Light is a form of energy, and, as we know, it travels in waves or ripples. Ordinary light waves spread out in all directions because the ripples are all jumbled. A laser unjumbles the waves and packs them side by side so that they all travel together. When light waves are packed together, they travel in a straight line instead of spreading out. These light waves make up a laser beam.

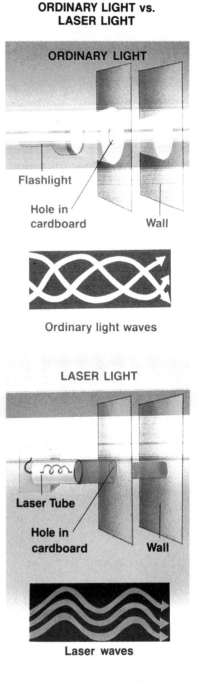

ORDINARY LIGHT vs. LASER LIGHT

ORDINARY LIGHT

Flashlight

Hole in cardboard

Wall

Ordinary light waves

LASER LIGHT

Laser Tube

Hole in cardboard

Wall

Laser waves

The flashlight beam and laser beam *both* go through the hole in a piece of cardboard, but the laser beam does not spread out.

39

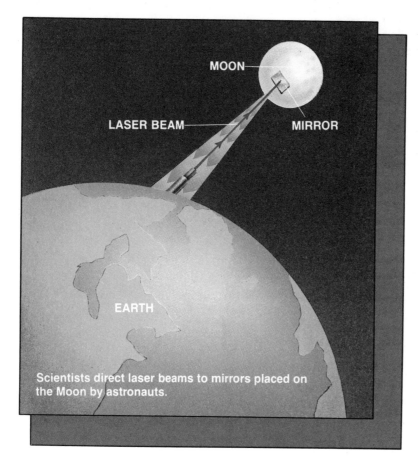

MOON

LASER BEAM

MIRROR

EARTH

Scientists direct laser beams to mirrors placed on the Moon by astronauts.

How do people use lasers?

Many uses have been found for lasers. Laser beams are much hotter than other light beams. Their heat can be used to weld or cut tiny things. Sometimes surgeons use a laser to perform delicate operations.

Laser beams can travel farther than other light beams. Scientists can measure how far it is from Earth to the moon by bouncing a laser beam off the moon.

What is a hologram?

A hologram is a picture that appears to have depth—just like the real object. When you see a normal picture, it looks flat. When you look at a hologram, the object looks so real you want to reach out and touch it! Holograms are made with lasers and photographic plates or film. You might find a hologram on a decal, in a magazine, or on one of your parents' credit cards.

This boy is looking at holographic art created with lasers.

40

You can't see it, and you can't touch it, but you can move through it. Sound and light waves travel through it, too. It's all around us, and it's called air. What is air? Charlie Brown and the *Peanuts* gang are here to reveal the mystery and magic of marvelous air.

THE AIR AROUND US

THE NATURE OF AIR

What is air?

Air is made up of gases. Gases are made up of very small particles called molecules. Molecules are always moving in different directions, bumping into things, but they are invisible to us. The two gases that make up most of the air are nitrogen and oxygen. Without the right amount of both gases, it would be difficult to breathe.

What happens when air molecules bump into each other, or collide?

When air molecules collide with walls or with each other, they create a force, or pressure. Air in a sealed box creates pressure against the walls of the box. If we make the box smaller, there are more collisions of air molecules, and the pressure increases.

CHANGING THE AIR'S TEMPERATURE

What is heat?

Heat is a form of energy. When we heat up air, we speed up the movement of the gas molecules. When we cool down air, we slow down the molecules.

How does a furnace make a whole house warm?

When coal, gas, or oil is burned inside a furnace, heat is produced. The heat can be moved from the furnace to other places in a house in at least three different ways:

1. The furnace can heat the air. A blower pushes the warm air from the furnace through tunnels called ducts. The ducts lead to openings in all parts of the house.

2. The furnace can heat water in a boiler. When the water boils, it turns to steam. The pressure of the steam makes it go through pipes to radiators in each room.

3. The furnace heats water in a boiler. A pump then sends the hot water through pipes to radiators. When the radiators become hot, they warm the air in the rooms.

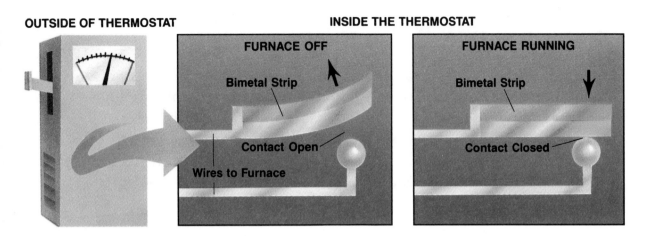

FURNACE OFF

Bimetal Strip

Contact Open

Wires to Furnace

FURNACE RUNNING

Bimetal Strip

Contact Closed

What makes a furnace turn on and off by itself?

Furnaces in houses and other buildings are controlled by thermostats (THUR-muh-stats). A thermostat turns the furnace on when the building is cool, and off when the building is warm. A thermostat has a bimetallic (by-muh-TAL-ick) spring made of two metal strips. *Bimetallic* means made from two metals.

When the room temperature rises, one of the metal strips winds up tighter than the other, and the spring stretches in one direction, turning off an electric switch. When the temperature falls, the spring stretches in the other direction, turning the switch back on.

HEY, WHO TURNED OFF THE HEAT?

What other things use thermostats?

Many things that work by heating or cooling use thermostats. Refrigerators, air conditioners, ovens, electric frying pans, and electric blankets all have thermostats. If you set an air conditioner's thermostat at 75 degrees Fahrenheit, it will keep the temperature of the room fairly steady. As soon as the air gets cooler than 75 degrees, the air conditioner shuts off. As soon as the air gets warmer than 75 degrees, the air conditioner turns on again.

How does a radiator warm a room?

A hot radiator warms the air next to it. The warmer the air gets, the lighter it becomes. Light air rises, so the warm, light air rises toward the ceiling. However, that does not leave airless space near the floor by the radiator because the gap is instantly filled by cool air that moves in from other parts of the room. This cool air becomes warm next to the radiator, and then *it* rises. The rising of the warm air and the movement of cool air toward the radiator is called convection (kun-VECK-shun). Convection is like a tiny wind that spreads the heat of the radiator all through the room.

What is solar heating?

Solar heating uses energy that comes from the sun. In recent years, oil and gas have become expensive. People have also realized that the burning of coal and oil pollutes the air and uses up natural resources that can never be replaced. So scientists and inventors have been searching for new ways to heat houses. One way is to capture heat from sunshine. Even in winter, a lot of heat comes to us in the form of waves from the sun. The problem is how to catch this heat energy and bring it indoors before it gets away.

How can people catch the sun's heat?

The most common solar heat collector is a low, flat box with a glass or plastic window on top. Most of the sun's light waves can pass easily through the glass or plastic. The inside of the box is painted black, because dark colors absorb, or soak up, the incoming light waves. Light colors reflect the waves.

IT'S NICE BEING THE FIRST ONE ON THE BLOCK WITH A SOLAR HOUSE.

The collector box is placed outdoors, usually on a roof facing the sun. The box is sealed tightly so that none of the heat that enters can get away. When the sun is shining, the box becomes hot inside, even in winter.

The next step is to bring the heat from the box into the house, using water pipes and a pump. Cool water is pumped from the house to pipes inside the collector box. The heat in the collector warms the water in the pipes. A pipe takes the hot water back into the house, where it is used. Sometimes the water goes into a storage tank, but if it stays there too long, it gets cold. Then it is pumped back up to the box to be reheated.

How does a dryer take the water out of wet laundry?

Wet clothes become dry because the water that is in them evaporates (ih-VAP-uh-rates). When water evaporates, it changes to water vapor, a kind of gas, and goes off into the air. A clothes dryer is a machine that makes evaporation take place quickly. It does this by blowing air on the clothes while they are tumbling around. Usually the air is warmed by a gas flame or an electric heater. This makes the water in the clothes evaporate quickly. Heat makes the tiny particles of water jump into the air. The moist air is then blown out of the dryer.

THERE'S NOTHING QUITE LIKE A WARM BLANKET, FRESH FROM THE DRYER.

What makes a refrigerator cold inside?

A refrigerator is a machine for taking heat out of a closed box. The working of a refrigerator is based on one special fact: a liquid absorbs, or soaks up, heat when it evaporates. When a liquid evaporates, it changes into a gas.

A refrigerator has a metal tube filled with a liquid called a refrigerant that evaporates fast. Part of the tube is inside the food box, and part of the tube is outside—underneath the refrigerator or on the back. If the inside of the food box gets warm, a thermostat turns on the refrigerator's motor. This makes the liquid flow through the tube. When the liquid enters the part of the tube that is *in* the food box, the liquid evaporates. It soaks up heat. Because the liquid has evaporated, the tube leading out of the food box is filled with gas. The tube leads to a compressor (come-PRESS-ur). A compressor pumps the gas into a condenser (cun-DEN-sir). As the gas flows through the condenser, it is changed into a liquid, and it gives off heat, so the condenser becomes hot. The heat goes into the air of the kitchen as the liquid moves through the part of the tube outside the refrigerator. The liquid again enters the food box. There, it evaporates and soaks up more heat.

How does an air conditioner make a room cool?

An air conditioner works exactly the same way as a refrigerator, but instead of taking heat out of a food box and putting it into the kitchen, an air conditioner takes heat out of a room and puts it outdoors.

Part of a room-sized air conditioner is inside a window. This part has a cold tube filled with a cooling liquid refrigerant. Part of the air conditioner is outside the window. This part has a compressor and a condenser tube that gives off heat. An air conditioner also has a fan that blows air past the cold tube and out into the room. In this way, an air conditioner takes the hot, humid air out of the room and returns cool, dry air to the room.

CHAPTER 6

What keeps the milk in your thermos cold and the hot chocolate warm? And what keeps your bicycle tires just right? The answer to the first question is: no air. The answer to the second question is: lots of air. Let's see why!

NO AIR AND LOTS OF AIR

ACUUMS

What is a vacuum?

When air is pulled out of a space so that no air is left, the empty space is called a vacuum (VACK-yoom).

How does a thermos bottle keep milk cold?

Thermos is a brand name for a vacuum bottle. A vacuum bottle works by insulating (IN-suh-late-ing) whatever you store in it. This means that when you store some-thing cold, like milk, the bottle lets in very little heat. When you store something hot, like cocoa, the bottle lets very little heat get out.

A vacuum bottle is built like a bottle inside of another bottle. There is a narrow space between the two bottles where the air has been pumped out to form a vacuum. The vacuum keeps air from touching the inside bottle. It is important to have no air between the two bottles. Air can carry heat to cold things and take heat away from hot things.

Some heat can get through a vacuum, but much of this heat is blocked by the bottle's shiny, silvery coating. Heat, which travels in waves, bounces off shiny, silvery things.

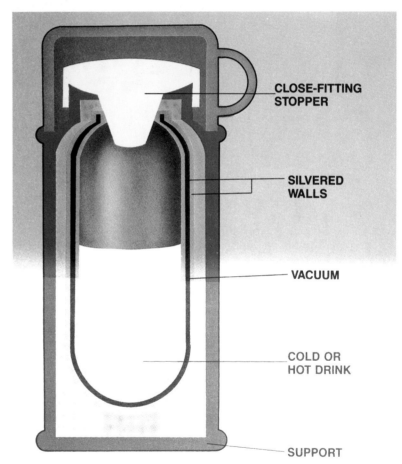

CLOSE-FITTING STOPPER

SILVERED WALLS

VACUUM

COLD OR HOT DRINK

SUPPORT

How did the vacuum cleaner get its name?

When a vacuum cleaner is turned on, a fan keeps blowing out most of the air from its tank. A space with only a little bit of air inside it is called a partial (PAR-shul) vacuum. As the air goes out of a vacuum cleaner's tank, a partial vacuum is left. That is why we call it a "vacuum" cleaner.

How does a vacuum cleaner pick up dirt?

It uses suction. The vacuum cleaner's fan blows air out of its tank or bag, leaving a partial vacuum inside. If you make an opening in the side of the container of a vacuum or partial vacuum, air will rush in to fill the empty space. This is called suction.

Along with the air that rushes into a vacuum cleaner come dust and dirt. The air is blown out again, but the dust and dirt are caught in the dust bag, which is made of paper or cloth. When the bag is full, you can throw it away or empty it and reuse it.

SORRY, PIGPEN. WE CAN'T PLAY INSIDE TODAY. MY MOTHER JUST VACUUMED.

COMPRESSED AIR AT WORK

How does a scuba-diving tank work?

The scuba tank holds compressed air. *Compressed* means that a lot is squeezed into a small space. If you let all the air out of a scuba tank, it could fill a whole room. On the tank, a special knob, called a valve, lets a little bit of air at a time go from the scuba tank through a hose to the diver's mouth.

The most important parts of a scuba outfit are the valves. They control the amount of gas or liquid that goes through a pipe or hose. Some valves are like faucets. They start or stop the flow of liquid or gas when you turn them with your hand. A special kind of valve in a scuba outfit automatically lets the diver get more air when he goes down deep. Another special valve lets the diver breathe used up air out into the water. It also doesn't let any water come in when the diver breathes in.

Who invented modern scuba equipment?

Ocean scientist Jacques Cousteau invented scuba gear.

It was invented in 1943 by Jacques Cousteau (ZHOCK koo-STOE), the famous French ocean scientist who has made many nature films for television. He didn't invent it all by himself, however. He had a partner named Emile Gagnan (ay-MEAL gah-NYAH). The two men made a perfect team. Cousteau was an ocean diver in the French navy. Gagnan was an engineer who knew a lot about valves.

Cousteau knew that old-fashioned diving equipment was unsafe. Often divers couldn't get enough air when they went down very deep. He saw that a new kind of valve was needed to control the amount of air coming from the scuba tank. Gagnan made the kind of valve Cousteau wanted.

What does scuba mean?

Scuba is an acronym made from the initials of the words *self-contained underwater breathing apparatus.*

What makes a fire extinguisher squirt?

Some fire extinguishers use compressed air to squirt out the water inside. As soon as the compressed air is given room, it will spread out. When a fire extinguisher is turned on, the compressed air pushes the water out the opening, which leads to a hose. The air goes out through the hose and pushes the water out.

Other fire extinguishers use compressed gas to make them squirt. The gas for most extinguishers, carbon dioxide, is pumped in at the factory. One type of extinguisher, however, makes compressed gas when you turn it upside down. This type is called a soda-acid extinguisher. The soda in soda-acid is not the kind you drink. It is a chemical called baking soda. The acid is a chemical called sulfuric (sull-FYOOR-ick) acid. The extinguisher is filled with water. Soda is dissolved in the water. In the top of the extinguisher is a small bottle of sulfuric acid. When you turn the extinguisher upside down, the acid mixes with water and baking soda. As a result, a lot of carbon dioxide gas is formed. It is under pressure inside the extinguisher until you let it out.

How does a fire extinguisher put out fires?

Fires need two things to keep going: a gas called oxygen, and fuel. Fuel is anything that can get hot enough to burn. Some extinguishers cool the fuel. Others keep oxygen in the air away from the fuel.

Extinguishers that squirt water work mostly by cooling the fuel until it is too cool to burn. Extinguishers that squirt carbon dioxide make the fuel very cold—colder than ice. They also drive oxygen away from the fire. Some extinguishers squirt a dry chemical powder. It forms a crust on the fuel. The crust keeps oxygen away from the fuel. Another type of extinguisher coats the fuel with foam. The foam keeps oxygen away from the fuel.

What machine is used to chop holes in the pavement?

Jackhammer, air hammer, and pneumatic (new-MAT-ick) drill are all names for the machine used to chop holes in sidewalks.

A jackhammer runs on compressed air. The air is pumped into the jackhammer through a hose. A trigger in the handle controls the flow of air.

Inside the jackhammer is a hollow tube called a cylinder (SILL-in-dur). Inside the cylinder is a piece of metal called a piston. The piston can slide up and down inside the cylinder.

When the jackhammer is turned on, air comes into the top of the cylinder. It pushes the piston down very hard. The piston then slams into a chisel that sticks out of the bottom of the jackhammer. The chisel is a pointed, metal bar. The hard blow of the piston drives the chisel into the pavement.

Next, the air comes into the *bottom* of the cylinder and pushes the piston back up. When the piston reaches the top of the cylinder, the air changes direction again. The piston goes down and slams into the chisel again. The piston goes up and down more than 1,000 times a minute! Each time the chisel chops away a piece of pavement.

Rock can be broken with the help of a jackhammer.

How does a bicycle pump work?

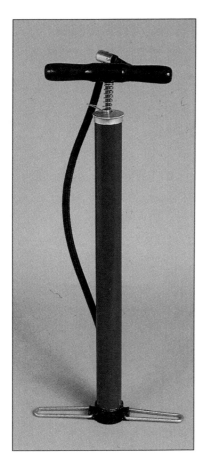

A bicycle pump compresses air. One common kind is made up of a handle, a cylinder, a valve, a hose, and a metal disk with a gasket around it. A gasket is a ring that fills an open space to make a pump or pipe leakproof. A gasket is sometimes made of rubber and sometimes of metal.

When you pull up on the handle of a bicycle pump, two things happen. First, the gasket hangs down loose and limp. This lets air go past it into the lower part of the cylinder. Second, the valve closes, so the air stays squeezed inside the bottom of the cylinder.

When you push down on the handle, the gasket presses tightly against the cylinder, making a tight seal. The air cannot get back up past the disk, but compressed air wants to spread out. Where can it go? When you push down on the handle, the valve opens. The air rushes out through the valve into the hose and then into your bicycle tire.

How does a car's brake pedal stop the car?

When a driver steps on a brake pedal, a chain of events begins. The pedal pushes a lever. The lever pushes a piston in a cylinder full of liquid. The piston pushes the liquid into four hoses. Each hose leads to one of the four wheels of the car. The liquid flows into a cylinder next to each wheel. There, the liquid pushes more pistons. These pistons push flat plates of metal against discs of metal called brake rotors. The rotors are attached to the wheels of the car. The plates of metal have layers of friction material called brake pads. The friction, or rubbing, of the pads slows down the turning of the wheels so that the car slows down and stops. When the brake pedal is released, the pads stop rubbing against the brake rotors.

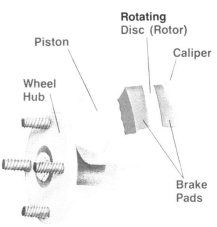

PARTS OF A BRAKE

Piston

Rotating Disc (Rotor)

Caliper

Wheel Hub

Brake Pads

56

Do trains have the same kind of brakes as cars?

Not exactly. Trains need very powerful brakes—much more powerful than brakes controlled by the pressure of one person pushing on one pedal with one foot. Train brakes use compressed air. The compressor is in the front of the train's locomotive. Hoses take the air to all the wheels. When the driver puts on the brakes, compressed air rushes into the hoses. The air pushes against some pistons. These pistons push curved pieces of metal against the wheels to slow down or stop their turning.

Big trucks use the same kind of brakes as trains.

What makes a car-lifting machine go up and down?

You have probably seen the machine used in service stations to lift a car into the air. It has a big, shiny metal tube that comes up out of the floor. That metal tube is really a giant piston. The piston fits into a pipe or cylinder buried in the floor. When the mechanic wants to lift the car, he turns on a pump. This pump uses compressed air to force liquid into the cylinder. The rising liquid pushes the piston up. When the car is raised high enough, the mechanic closes a valve. This keeps the liquid in the cylinder. The liquid keeps the piston from sliding back down into the floor. Then the mechanic turns off the pump. Now it is safe for him to go under the car and fix it. The car can't fall as long as liquid stays in the cylinder. When the mechanic wants to let the car down, he opens the valve. The liquid slowly leaves the cylinder and goes into a storage tank. As the liquid leaves the cylinder, the piston slowly sinks to the floor.

DID YOU KNOW...?

WHY WOULD ANYONE WANT TO WHISPER?

• The average light bulb lasts for 750 to 1,000 hours. A light bulb made by the Shelby Electric Company in 1901 still burns when switched on, almost 90 years after first being turned on.

...AND NOW, MY IMPRESSION OF A BEAGLE.

• Have you ever put your hands in front of the light of a movie projector and made funny rabbit and alligator shadow figures? Those shadows show us that light travels in straight lines. When your hand blocks the light, it creates a shadow. If light traveled in curves, it would curve around your hand, and you would see no shadow at all.

• Imagine a room shaped like an egg! People have built elliptical, or egg-shaped, rooms because of what such rooms do to sound. In these rooms, a person can whisper at one end, and someone standing in a special spot across the room can hear very clearly what is being said. People standing anywhere else in the room cannot hear the whisper at all! The Statuary Hall of the U.S. Capitol was built like this and is called the "whispering gallery."

- There's a world of light and color inside a kaleidoscope (kall-EYE-duh-skope). This long tube is filled with loose scraps of colored glass, plastic, or paper. What makes a kaleidoscope magical, however, are the angled mirrors inside. When light shines on them, the mirrors reflect a pattern of color that changes every **time the colored pieces** move. If you want to see a new pattern, all you need to do is turn the kaleidoscope!

- The Pontiac Silverdome is a Michigan sports stadium with an amazing roof. It's held up by air pressure! Five pounds per square inch support the Fiberglas™ roof.

- Did you ever wonder how whipped cream comes out of the can? Inside a spray can is compressed gas. The compressed gas is always pushing at the cream, but it can't rush out until you push the button on top of the can. Pressing the button is like opening a faucet. You give the compressed gas a place **to go. As the gas** rushes out, it pushes out the whipped cream. The fancy ridges come from the can's star-shaped nozzle.

- People who visited the Washington Monument on July 17 and 18 in 1987 were treated to a super sound event. David Frank of Toronto, Canada, whistled there for 35 hours—nonstop!

THAT'S MUSIC TO MY EARS!

IN THE

NEXT VOLUME

Have you ever wondered how a star is born, or what the weather is like on Neptune, or where a black hole is found? You can find the answers to these questions and lots more in volume 9, *Our Incredible Universe— From Stars to Black Holes.*